TH
PASSIONATE
LOVER

THE
PASSIONATE
LOVER
HOW TO KEEP YOUR RELATIONSHIP ALIVE

JOE TANGO

Outskirts Press, Inc.
Denver, Colorado

The Passionate Lover
How To Keep Your Relationship Alive

Outskirts Press, Inc.
http://www.outskirtspress.com

ISBN: 978-1-4327-4779-4

Outskirts Press and the "OP" logo are trademarks belonging to Outskirts Press, Inc.

PRINTED IN THE UNITED STATES OF AMERICA

INTRODUCTION

This book is written for men. The purpose is to help you with the key principles needed to pursue your goal as a better husband, a better man, and the passionate lover your woman is looking for. How can you raise a woman's libido and sexually stimulate her mind and her body? How can you make her fantasize about being with you? Let this be your mission to read and apply these simple principles to your life and your relationship.

Allow this course to be the blueprint that you follow straight to successful intimacy in your life. This book was written as a collection of short, true inspirational stories to motivate you to improve your self-image and your love life. This collection of stories is meant to teach you to change your mind-set from negative behavior and thoughts to more positive behavior and thoughts. This is a crucial step in a successful marriage or relationship, and will ultimately teach you how to be a more passionate, hot lover. Read true short stories of real people I have helped throughout my life. I hope you will find something in this book that will help you.

TAKE MY EXPERIENCE WITH YOU

I am Joe Tango. I have been a Latin and ballroom dance instructor since 1985. I am not a doctor, nor do I have a PhD. I want you to think of me as someone who has years of "on the job training" experience. What you are getting from me is truthful insights into life experiences from the dance floor. I am passing on to you what I have learned about women. I did not go to school for this. What you read here are the facts, however subjective they may be… this is life as I've lived it and I am here to share what I know.

For years women have been asking how they can get their husband or boyfriend to be the hot, passionate lover they fantasize about. They can't understand how to improve their love life or why their sex drive for their husband or boyfriend ceases to exist. Women ask me repeatedly what they can do to make their boyfriend or husband become a passionate lover.

I am sure you are wondering how I know so much about women and being a passionate lover. My experience as a dance instructor has given me the opportunity to be with lots of women, friends and lovers, both married and single. But my familiarity with women started much earlier than that. Allow me to give you some background.

I was the last son of nine children, consisting of five brothers and four sisters. I was a sickly child. I stayed at home a great deal, but my brothers did not like to play with me because they were afraid I would get sick and die. I was left to play with my sisters and their girlfriends, from the time I was a little boy until my late teens. Even then, at a very young age, I remember girls asking me things about guys, especially their boyfriends.

ONLY GUY AT
HER PAJAMA PARTY

When my sisters and their girlfriends had a pajama party, I would be the only boy there. I played games with the girls, brushing their hair and telling stories. I was always listening to the girls as they told me all about their boyfriends. The conversation always turned to what they liked and wanted in guys.

I could see how girls grew and matured faster than boys. In their minds they were thinking like grown women. Wow, these girls were talking about kissing, holding hands, lovemaking, getting married, and having babies. The boys at this age, on the other hand, were out in the yard looking for bugs and playing with dirt. You can see that my four sisters aided me in developing an ever-increasing knowledge of what girls think about and focus on. The experiences they exposed me to left a deep impression on my heart and in my mind.

My experiences have been very beneficial to me as an

adult, more than all the other experiences I ever had in my life. This is why I am capable of helping you. Moreover, I can teach you how to change your way of thinking from I can't do this to Yes I can. I can teach you to have a definite goal and defined aim, to be more successful with your love life, your marriage, your relationships, and the way you are living.

I have been called upon for years to help men and women put the passion back into their love and sex lives. There should be no disappointment reading and understanding what is in this book or applying this to change your love and sex life.

THE
PASSIONATE LOVER

This book is for men who are married or in a relationship where you two are bored with your love and sex life
because the fire and passion are gone, or because years of
lame sex have made her subconscious mind object to sex,
and as a result she has lost her interest in having any sex
with you at all. Alternately, at night when you two go to
bed, you are hoping and praying she will want sex from
you, but when you turn and touch her she rejects any, and
all, of your advances.

She knows having sex with you is always the same thing,
without change, and, in fact, she knows it's going to be
boring again. It's like a pattern has been set; you are now
on a treadmill and going in circles.

Now if you are looking to improve your love and sex life
and put the ahh! back into your relationship, then read on.
Or if you are looking to have your wife or girlfriend begging you to have hot, passionate sex with her and ripping

off your clothes to make hours of love to you, then read on.

Time to wake up

Think of this book as a sexual awakening for your love life. This book is not for you if you are going through a divorce or you two are splitting up. It is a little too late. But if you two are willing to work and apply what I have in this book, it just might work.

This book is not to show you how to pick up girls or how to get laid. This book is to wake you up and to help you. If you are willing to change yourself first, and you have a definite aim to make your marriage and relationships work, this book will teach you how to please your woman and be her hot, passionate lover.

How you can raise her libido and sexually stimulate her mind and her body? How you can make her fantasize about being with you all day long and receiving pleasure beyond anything she has ever imagined? It's all up to you to change yourself to make it work. Yes, it is time for a change, and it starts with you.

THINKING OF WHAT YOU WILL HAVE

I have a woman friend who was telling me how bad her love and sex life are. She told me she had been married over twenty years and that she and her husband had not engaged in sex in over sixteen years. We'll refer to this couple as Dave and Tina. Tina told me that there was no chemistry between them anymore. As I listened to Tina, she went on to tell me how Dave would spend hours and hours just watching television. She said he didn't even know she was alive.

As I sat in their home talking with her, all I could hear from her was how bad her life was and how she was missing the love, the passion, and the sexual excitement in her life. She was a nice-looking woman. She was small in stature and very well kept.

JUST STOP TALKING, LET'S FIX IT

Every time I told Tina what she could do to help fix her problem, she would go back to saying over and over again how bad things were in her marriage. Instead of thinking of what she could have in her husband, Dave, she was holding onto the negative and what she did not have in her marriage.

I could see she was attracting into her life the things she was thinking about and holding onto. We need to understand that our mind is the most powerful tool we have. I told her that what you think about, you bring about and draw to you.

All she was doing was holding onto what she did not want in her life. I told her to change her mind-set and stop thinking of what she did not have and think of what she could have. I asked her, "How can your husband enjoy your company if you do not enjoy your own company?"

She replied by saying, "I have been crying out for years for some sexual excitement from my husband, Dave. I want him to take charge in our bedroom, take care of my sexual needs, and give me the stimulation that I crave as a woman." She proceeded to tell me how clumsy and clueless her husband was in the bedroom and how she couldn't say anything to him because it would bruise his ego. She said she did not want to risk hurting his feelings, so she just fantasized about being with another man. I told her that she needed to focus on what she had, not what she didn't have. I said, "Think about what you appreciate about your husband. Moreover, you will see things change in him."

THE TV ZOMBIE

As I was sitting in the living room, I saw her husband, Dave, a somewhat overweight man looking way out of shape. He was sitting in his old recliner chair, like his favorite blue jeans that he did not want to depart from. His eyes were glazed over as he stared, zombie-like, deep into his television. I don't even think he was aware of his surroundings. I watched as he tightened his hold on the remote, squeezing in fear that someone would touch it or he might miss something on TV.

I could see how it was an invisible barrier that Dave had put up between his wife and himself. It was as if he was saying to her, "I do not want to sit with you. I want to sit by myself, just me, my chair, and my TV in my own little world. I'm the king of the remote."

Now, a recliner chair is nice to have as a single man, but if you have that special someone in your life they might see it as a wall between the two of you. Try something fun and get a recliner chair that seats two.

As I was talking with Dave, he told me that he couldn't bear the thought of seeing his wife with another man. He was telling me that their sex life was boring, explaining that it was the "same ol' kind of thing." Dave said, "I used to ask Tina for sex all the time. Then it got to where I would even beg and plead for it. I would get so frustrated with myself that I didn't even feel like a man." I said to Dave, "The one thing I know that will ruin any man's sex life is not to give his wife or girlfriend an orgasm, whether it is vaginal or clitoral."

Many women I have been with have told me that they never had orgasms in intercourse with their husband for years during their marriage. They get so bored that they will fake an orgasm just so their husband will stop, and sex will be over. Dave said that he got tired of asking and begging his wife, Tina, for sex; therefore he just stopped. I told Dave that it appeared to me that sex was all about him and what he was getting. I asked him, "What's in it for Tina? The reason you have to ask and beg Tina for sex is you are not satisfying her sexual needs in bed. You do nothing to satisfy her. Look at it from her perspective. Why would she or any woman want to have sex with you at all? You get yours and she gets nothing out of it."

In fact, she will fake an orgasm just to get it over with. This is why a woman will lose all interest in having sex with her husband/boyfriend. Worst of all, as a result, she will seek it elsewhere.

DO NOT FORGET TO KISS

I asked Dave, "Do you two kiss?" He said, "Yes, hmmm? Well, sometimes when I go to work." I asked Dave again, "Do you two kiss like you are in love, and when was the last time you kissed her intimately? I'm talking about you going up to her and caressing her body and passionately kissing her for half a minute, then looking deep into her eyes and telling her how much you love her." Dave quickly replied, "J.T., it's been years."

Women love kissing. For women, there is no better turn on for her than hot, passionate, romantic kissing. Don't get too crazy at first with the tongue action. Slowly add passionate kissing. The best thing to do is slow down and take your time.

Don't try to thrust your tongue in your partner's mouth. Simply press your lips against hers, giving her a light kiss to start, and then start French kissing her. Insert your tongue deep into her mouth and slowly begin dancing with your partner's tongue. Then put your hand to the back of her head and pull her tightly to you as you kiss her lips.

Go to any restaurant that gives you poor service and bad food, and I can guarantee that you will not go back for more of the same service. Your woman is no different. If you give her poor service in bed, do you think she will want more from you? I told Dave to take charge of her in the bed and stop asking her for sex.

Take your time, make plans for a night of steamy romance, and give her the hot, passionate sex she's been craving.

DOMINATE HER
IN THE BEDROOM

This is what we are missing today from marriages and relationships. Stop being the little boy in the bedroom. Sometimes women want their men to be more dominant and take charge of their sexual needs. Women are looking for a man in the bedroom, not a wimp or a little boy. Your woman needs to feel that you are confident in the bedroom. Be the bad boy and make the sex incredibly exciting for her.

Your job is to satisfy her in bed, giving her sexual satisfaction without causing any discomfort or pain. You want to take her far beyond anywhere she has ever imagined with any man in the bedroom. While some women like to be dominant, others do not. This is why communication of the do's and don'ts in the bedroom are very important. Some women also like the missionary position, which is a good display of dominance from the man.

TAKE ACTION
IN THE BEDROOM

This position is perfect if you want complete control over her. Tuck a pillow under her hips so that she will get deeper penetration from you. Fold her knees toward her chest and rest her calves on your back to allow you to go deeper.

This can aid you in giving her a deeper orgasm. Your partner will feel you going deeper with the missionary position. This is where you can be more dominant toward her. You can put both hands under her hips, and this will help you to give her a more intense penetration. As you are thrusting deeper into her, you can whisper to her a little something dirty, raising her libido as you are stimulating her mind at the same time.

You are giving her more than just sex; this will be incredible to her. It offers her full, deep vaginal orgasms in intercourse. This is what women want when they are making love. Your aim is to be so incredibly exciting that she will become addicted to having sex with you all the time. She will have an addiction to your sex and nothing else will compare.

IT TAKES TWO

Dave said to me, "How, J.T.? I don't know where, or even how, to start over." Now, as it takes two to tango, the same holds true for a good marriage or relationship. When you two were first dating you had great communication with each other. You had so much in common, and you would make time for each other. You two were a team. You would think and daydream about each other, making plans together, just to have that special night. Now it's like you are in two different worlds. I asked Dave if he would be willing to start over and, moreover, get it back again.

Primarily, before you do anything at all, you, as the man, must change yourself. You must move from the negative world you built for yourself and change your life. Stop thinking and talking about the negative. Start by communicating with each other.

It must start with you. Tell her it's over and make your stand—no more will you be begging for sex, because it's time for you two to tango by setting aside lovemaking time. Talk to her about making time for hot, passionate sex. Get her to work with you on this. If you can spend four to six hours looking at TV, you can use that time for her and hot, passionate sex. She will not mind. But always remember, SEX NEVER STARTS IN THE BEDROOM.

Set your goal to make her feel like a woman again, giving her a night with clitoris stimulation and deep vaginal orgasms. Unfortunately, a lot of men don't understand or even have a clue that women love and want GOOD (INCREDIBLE) SEX, and they want it as much, if not more, than men want sex. Women are extremely sexual, much more sexual than men, who want any kind of sex from whomever they can get it. Now, a woman is smart and meticulous; she's looking for that one man who knows how to give her incredible sex.

Think of this: if you will always give her deep, incredible orgasms every time you have sex with her, she will always want more from you. Moreover, when you give her really incredible, deep stimulation, she can't get enough of it.

She will be begging you for sex, with you giving her deep vaginal orgasms, and ripping off your clothes just to get it from you. I can say this is true from my own experience with the women I have been with and the ability to give a woman deep vaginal orgasms in sex every time by being a passionate lover.

BE WILLING TO CHANGE YOU

You must be willing to change yourself first. If you have a low libido, and it's hard for you to get stimulated or you cannot get an erection, then see your doctor. One thing to do is look at yourself in a mirror and ask yourself if you'd want to have sex with you. Adjusting to the ever varying and changing times, there are so many things you can do to improve yourself.

If you are overweight go to the gym, clean yourself up. If your hair has too much gray, dye it. The little things will add up. Shower more than once a week, and stop wearing the same old clothes. Get active because no woman wants to see her man being lazy and doing nothing to improve himself. One of the biggest things men will do after we get married or live with a woman is WE GET LAZY.

I cannot say this enough. Unfortunately, for years you have seen her as a mother, a cook, or just a housecleaner. As time went by, the excitement you had in your relationship disappeared. I hope this course will inspire and motivate you to be more serious-minded before your relationship comes to its end. You need to change your mind-set and to see her as your girlfriend. You can start by dating her again.

NO SMOKING!!!

The most important thing you need to work on first is always you. Go shower and clean up, and if you have a nice man's perfume/fragrance, put it on. If you are a smoker, do not smoke! Let her smell a clean and fresh you.

A smoker's breath is a big turn-off! You are looking to get intimate and stimulate her. The last thing she needs to smell is your bad breath. I have been out with very beautiful women who are smokers, and each time we would kiss, or I would smell her hair or her body, it was a big turn-off to me. I had couples who were both smokers and said to me, "Even as a smoker we still like to smell a nice clean body."

Moreover we do not go to school for this. We learn it on our own. If you learn good or bad habits, that is how you act. One out of every hundred men is a very passionate lover.

GIRLFRIEND AND NOT YOUR WIFE

It is easier to get out of a dating relationship than if you two are married. Just pack up your things and move out. If you are married, it will take a lot more to end your marriage. You have lawyer fees, court costs, and counseling, selling of this, selling of that, who will keep this, who will keep that. Thousands of dollars going out, child support, alimony, it never ends. To avoid this, many changes need to be made in your life. This is why you do not need the attitude of I do not care. I am married, so she won't go anywhere. Why work to keep her?

DATING YOUR WIFE

Stop seeing her as your wife, where you don't need to work to keep her. Let me suggest to you if you can see her as your girlfriend this will enable you to keep trying to win her love and enjoy your close personal friendship. If she is your girlfriend/wife and you two have been together for years, then see her as a new girlfriend. Basically, you need to woo her and win her love again.

This will give you two the opportunity to fall back in love. A good way to start is take her out on a date night. Don't do it just one time and then think you fixed it. You need to do it again and again, putting the same energy into keeping her love that you put into trying to win her over. There is so much you two can do to have fun.

Go to the shopping mall or a park, walk and hold her hand and talk to each other. Do what you would do if you two were starting to date.

Communication is so very important with any marriage or relationship. You want to start all over again. You do not want to wait until she's about to walk out the door and you are on your knees begging her not to go. If you are telling her you will do anything not to lose her, then it's too late. Do it now! Do not wait until you realize she's unhappy to be with you. Then you hear the slamming of the door. Now, if you're smart, it won't happen.

You want to woo her again just as if you were trying to win her love. It's your job to turn things around because this is why men and women will look for excitement outside of the home. I cannot say this enough. It's your job to keep the excitement at home with her.

HAVING A DATE NIGHT

Go out and have fun with a little dinner, some wine, and dancing. Hold her passionately in your arms or go see a movie. These things would be a nice way to start something new. Enjoy being a couple and start falling in love again. See her as your date and a century's woman.

You should make the first move. One of the things you can do is start kissing her. This should not be a quick little kiss on the lips that says, "Hey, dear, how was your day?" You can start by being romantic and giving her a passionate French kiss.

Yes, kiss her tenderly and passionately for about 30 seconds daily. Give her an "I love you" kiss and caress her body, holding it to yours daily, not when you are horny and it's time for you to get yours. Do new things to keep her from being bored with you.

One of the things I enjoy doing is giving my woman lots of stimulating foreplay. First, I will stimulate her mind as I whisper the things I will do to her body. This is giving her mental pictures of us. The things I will be doing to her that I know she likes.

Then I will be her bad boy. As I push her against the wall I'm holding her by the back of her head, and her hair, being a little rough the way I know she likes it. Then I'm kissing her neck, her ears, and whispering the things I know she likes to hear from me.

Being in total control of her body, I run my fingers down between her legs, giving her stimulating foreplay and raising her libido. I can feel her body responding as she quivers to my every touch. Again, this is why I know communication is very important with any, and all, relationships. I know how far I can go.

This will work if—and only if—you two will work with it.

CHANGE YOUR MIND-SET

Moreover, think and talk, and move toward the positive. It's easier than we think. For example, picture yourself driving down a long road and someone is in front of you driving very slowly. Let's say they are on the cell phone now, and it is getting you upset and mad and making you think negatively. Change your mind-set to: I am so happy I can drive, I have a car, and I can go around the person in front of me. Then put them out of your mind and don't think of them anymore because it's over and be happy you have something to drive. Some people do not even have a car.

Think of the Law of Attraction with the things that are going on now in your life and your marriage. You have attracted these things to you. Whatever you are giving thought about, you will bring about. You will bring it into your life.

YOU ARE A MAGNET

Whether it is bad, or it is good, you will draw it to yourself. If you focus upon something you do not want, this is what you will pull into your life. Just like a magnet, this is what you will draw to yourself.

If all you can think about is how bad your marriage, your love, or your sex life is and how bad you feel, and what you two don't have in your life, then this is what you are pulling into your life. Stop holding on to what you don't want in your marriage and your love life, and let it go.

Replace it with what you do want: a happy marriage, happy relationship, a car, money. Think as if you have it now. Make a list. Write down all the good, positive things you want in your marriage and in your love life to change, and see it as if you had it already.

Think, and talk, and feel, and move toward the positive. It's very important to feel the positive. You will see things coming into your life.

SEE MYSELF LIVING
IN THIS HOUSE

One day I was looking to buy a three-bedroom home. The Realtor said there was no way I would ever get the house I had been looking at because my credit score was too low. As a dance instructor you have no way to prove your income. Now, this did not let me down as I walked through my home—yes, I said my home!

I could see myself living in this house as we walked through the house. I was touching the walls, saying, "I'm so happy this is my home." I was holding on to the reality of moving in my home before January 20, 2007. I had even set a date to move in. Well, on January 18, 2007, I did move in.

I was holding on to the things I want in my life. If you can see it in your mind's eye, you will hold it in your hand. As I walked into the house, I was feeling good about having this house. As you can see, I stayed focused on buying this house.

I had a definite chief aim and this house was it, and I did get the home that I wanted. I was focused on buying this house and getting it to be my home—this house was my definite chief aim.

POSITIVE THOUGHT BRINGS POSITIVE THINGS

You will see the change coming into your life. You will be drawing into your life the positive things you are looking for in your marriage and love life.

I had a friend who was telling me how the police were always after him. When he went out driving in his car, the police would pull him over. If he went to the store, the police would follow him; when the police had a road check, he would be the car that would be pulled over.

As you can see, he was drawing all this to himself. I told him to stop seeing the police as if they were after him and start seeing the police as if they were his friends, out to help him, not after him. He was attracting into his life the negative. What he did not want was what he was bringing into his life. He was drawing this to his life.

I told him to stop focusing on what he did not want in his life and focus on what he did want, and it would happen because he would unconsciously draw it to him.

If you are holding onto the bad and the negative things in your life, with the same energy you can turn it around and consciously draw the positives to you and your life.

TALK TO HER, NOT AT HER

I was teaching a couple whom I will refer to as Josh and Debbie. They had been married for ten years. Debbie asked me how they could put the passion and the fire back into their cold and dying marriage. I could not get over how they talked at each other, not to each other.

All I heard from these two students were negative comments to and about each other. They put each other down over and over again as if I was not there, yet I was being asked to help put the passion and the fire back in their marriage by the wife.

I told Josh that being a passionate lover is from the inside out. First, you need to work on you. It all starts with you as the man, who you are, before you ever start. When a couple is always fighting or putting each other down, they are putting up walls of negativity between them. You need to know how to communicate without any of the negative.

The two of you should make it a rule never to put each

other down, or say anything out of the way to or about each other. I told Josh that positive thoughts would bring positive things. Change your mind-set from the negative and watch what happens. Then the door can and will open for you. To be a passionate lover you must be willing to start over with you.

This will open the door for new things to come into your life; then you will see a whole new world open before your eyes. You will see a new world that I have seen for years.

OUT WITH THE OLD

Men generally think that there is no way to have great sex. The man will start by fondling her, or, shall we say, groping her. This is not the pleasure she's looking for because this is more to stimulate him. Then he will just go straight to intercourse without even stimulating her by just sticking it in and going for it... Wrong!

How can we as men misunderstand something that is such a blessing? This is why women can say no so fast to a man and think all men are jerks. It's because of men having the "stick it in and go for it" attitude.

We need to stop doing the same old thing we've been doing for years. The attitude that has put us, as men, in the place where women are saying all men are the same must change. Most men don't even know how to begin to be romantic, or where to start. There's no passion, no stimulation, no foreplay.

STEP INTO HER SEX LIFE

You need to think as a woman... Yes, think as a woman. Ask yourself if you give her sexual excitement, and are you stimulating her body, and her mind, before you ever take her to the bedroom? Putting yourself in her place, you see sex as if it's all the same old thing. Let's say you never had an orgasm with her at all. You go to bed, she gives you some kissing, a little touch here, a little touch there, you are not fully hard or erect, and she puts you inside of her and starts riding you, moaning and groaning.

Now you hear her saying in your ear, "Oh, oh baby," and she is done and it's all over. Then she gets up and walks away, leaving you all alone in the bedroom, lying on your back. You are erect and she is gone and you get nothing. You are in bed thinking she will be back just to kiss you, but she's all done and she's not coming back to you. Sex is over for you, until she needs more sex from you. You know she is a very loving, caring woman. You know she would do anything for you, but she does not take care of your sexual needs.

When you do take her into the bedroom, you do not give her any foreplay, you do not stimulate her at all, 30 seconds into the sex and it is all over for you—she gets nothing. You made her feel as if she is just a place for you to dump your sperm.

This is why women see men as all the same. Men are just looking to thrust it in and pull out, get theirs, and move on. You don't even take five minutes to hold her after you are done, and you call this your love and sex life. All that is left is for you to stand at the foot of the bed, beat your chest, and yell like Tarzan.

DON'T BE HER BAD APPLE

So ask yourself, would you go to the store to buy an apple and take a big bite from it just to see if it is full of worms? Would you bite into that same apple again? Are you the kind of man in the bedroom that women will be talking about for days? Study yourself and do your homework on you.

Find out what your motive is and what inspires you to perform. Is it just to get yours, to have your orgasm? I want you to refrain from performing just for you, and think of performing just for her. Something I always enjoy doing is seeing just how many orgasms I can give my partner before I get mine.

Your first goal for yourself would be to satisfy her sexual needs and to slow down, take your time with her. Make plans ahead. No woman wants you to rush and get it over. Use the fundamental principles to apply to your love and your sex life.

Stop doing the things you have been doing that are not

working for you, and do what will work. You will have her coming back to you again—and again, repeatedly. This is what you need in your life, to be that passionate lover. You will be the one she has been looking for all of her life to have super sex with, and a love life with the one she loves.

A NEW MAN,
DESIRE TOMORROW

Think of a little boy playing in his clubhouse with his toys. Two years ago, the little boy got a new GI Joc for Christmas; he played and played with his GI Joe when the toy was new. But that was two years ago.

One day the little boy from next door came over to play and saw GI Joe lying over in the corner of the clubhouse. He picked up the doll to play with it. Wow, GI Joe was dirty and his leg was off, over against the wall, all of his clothes were gone, and someone had taken a pen and marked all over GI Joe's face. Joe looked bad, as if he lost the war.

Poor GI Joe. The little boy who got Joe for Christmas two years ago thought it was his best Christmas toy ever, but now the little boy is bored with GI-Joe, so he gives his toy no attention.

The little boy next door picked up the toy and started playing with it. Then he took the GI Joe doll home and his mom fixed and cleaned the doll.

GI Joe looked good, all cleaned up with a new leg, new clothes, and a clean face. Wow, GI Joe looked new, and the little boy played with Joe day and night.

IS SHE YOUR GI JOE

Now GI Joe has a new friend who will care for him, play with him, and give him the attention he has been waiting for. As you can see, what the little boy was doing is what we do with the ones we love, after being in a relationship for years or being married.

The last thing you ever want is for the woman in your life to be bored in bed with you. The woman in our life we are bored with today will be a new man's passion and desire tomorrow. It is up to you to keep the fire and the passion going. Don't throw it away to be taken by another man.

TIME TO SET YOUR PLANS

Are the things you are doing now in your love and sex life working? Are you giving her an earth-shattering night of hot, passionate sex, better than she has ever had with you? Do not be embarrassed to say or to admit that you are not.

Change what is not working to what will work for her and for you. I want you to have the brains enough to understand the full significance of what you are about to learn from me in this book.

Therefore, if you want things in your life to change, you need first to change the things in your life. It starts with you. As men, we need to know how to set the mood. This is the most important part of being a good lover. As a dance instructor, through my years of experience with women, I cannot tell you how important it is for her. To have you as a man, to take your time, make your plans, to give her a night of steamy romance and hot, passionate sex is one of the biggest things in the mission today in forming lasting relationships and marriages.

FANTASIES IN
THE BEDROOM

In your relationship, you need to ask her to tell you about her fantasies. Let her know you are genuinely curious about her.

Let her know you will not judge her at all; tell her you will completely accept her fantasies, and you have a deep appreciation for her and her fantasies. You need to do this in the context of demonstrating your deep appreciation for her and any and all of her fantasies.

One thing, do not push her to tell you; she will appreciate your understanding. Our biggest fear is that she will tell you about being with another man. What I have seen and from the women I have talked to is that their fantasies are about their husbands or their boyfriends.

I had a student who told me her fantasies were of her husband. She had been married for 15 years. She told me about her fantasies, which she had been having for years. She said she was always afraid to tell her husband, thinking he would not appreciate her or be interested in anything to do with her or her fantasies.

HER HUSBAND
WAS HER FANTASY

Her fantasy was to go to a bar and play pool. At that time her husband would come into the bar, dressed in slacks and a dress shirt, wearing a nice tie, and then he would place his money on the pool table.

She would buy him a cold beer. As they played pool, she would walk over to him, slowly and very sexy, and take off his tie, kiss his lips, and walk away to get both of them a shot of rum. As they took their shot together she would passionately kiss him. Then she would undo his shirt and kiss his chest. She would take him by the hand, walk out of the bar, and have hot, passionate, wild sex in his car. This was the fantasy she'd had for years about her husband.

One of the biggest mistakes I have seen from men today is they will be with a woman for years and never know about their fantasies or sharing them with her. I cannot say to you enough how important communication is, in order to know her.

UNLEASH HER FANTASIES

You should be comfortable with her in your relationship where you can just ask her. Therefore, you will know what to say and what you can do to sexually arouse and stimulate her. This is the excitement she's looking to get from you. Again, it all goes back to you.

This is easily done, just by asking her to tell you about her fantasies and how you can fulfill them for her. How would you like to hear from her and her friends how you were the one to make her fantasies come true?

You can start by saying to her, "Honey, I want to fulfill your deepest, darkest desires in our bedroom. I want to be your hot, passionate lover. I want to be the one to unleash your fantasies beyond any of your wildest dreams in our bedroom."

Ask her to tell you what she fantasizes about. What really turns her on in the bedroom? If she says, "I want to be your slut in the bedroom. I want you to control and dominate me in bed," then you must always respect her as a woman. Keep in mind she's your wife or girlfriend; it would be better for you to fulfill her fantasies and her deepest desires than for her to have someone else fulfill them.

Then you need to act on them and take care of her needs. She will remember you for years to come. It is very important for any relationship to keep your communication with one another open. This will help you with your plans for any night of hot, passionate sex.

SUPER BOWL PARTY WITHOUT STIMULATION

It is just like having a Super Bowl party without making plans. Paul and Joe are two guys who are each having a Super Bowl party. Paul had chips, beer, and dip for his friends. Joe went all out, working all day to make his party a success. He had hamburgers, hot dogs, beer, cold drinks, chips, dip, and the works.

Joe called all his friends two weeks before the big game. He asked them to wear their favorite team shirt. Now which party will go over big with the friends? As you can see, Joe took the time to make plans.

Do you see how Joe set the mood? He made plans for his event. He took his time to set the mood. We need to set the mood hours or even days before ever thinking of taking her to the bedroom. Slow down, make your plans, enjoy, and have fun.

Some women can take up to 30 minutes to get wet for

you or even to have their first orgasm. Now as men, we need to slow down and put our speed on a low boil. She needs stimulating first before you ever have intercourse.

HE KNOWS HOW TO TREAT HER

Have you ever seen a guy who had lots of women always hanging all over him, always calling him and taking him out? Now, he is an average-looking man, not a big six-foot-tall guy or a muscle-bound man.

This man knows how to talk and set the mood. These women know he will make plans just for them. They know this man knows how to treat them as a woman. He knows how they want to be treated. This guy will go all out just to make his woman have an earth-shattering night of hot, passionate sex.

He knows how to make her feel comfortable. He will take great care and planning with candles, the music, the wine, and slow dancing in his living room, getting her to laugh. This woman is thinking he is not like all the other boring guys because he makes her feel special and in fact he is lots of fun.

This is all about you not being the same boring man, and

showing her something new. This is what women have been crying out for years. As men, we tend to get lazy after being married or in a relationship for a few years. As much as she loves you, she can and she will become bored with you and the things you are doing.

STARTING OVER

Now, with your wife or your girlfriend, before you ever take her to bed, makes plans hours or even days ahead to set the mood. Just like when you two were first dating, you would make things just right for her, like the music, the flowers, your cologne, the food, your drinks. Everything had to be just right, and you would do all you could just to make her happy.

You would do anything for her. So why does it need to stop after you two are married or you've been together for years?

Keep this in mind. The same fire and passion you had with her before, you can have again. You can, and you will, have it again, but it is up to you to keep it going.

Think of it as starting over. This is why after being with someone for some time, the fun, the excitement, and the passion are gone. This is why a woman will get sexual frustration in their relationship and lose any interest in having sex with you. You are no longer trying to keep it alive. You can start over by adding and doing new things.

Trying new things is not that hard to do. It takes just a little of your time, and make it fun. You can go to the store and buy one or two red roses and pick off the petals to put all over the sheets and the pillows. Have three or four candles lit, nice chilled white wine, and soft music. It's the little things you are doing that add the spark to the boring love and sex life. You must keep it alive because it's like anything—if you don't use it you will lose it.

TO THE KITCHEN

Let us take it to the kitchen. Did you know food is very erotic if you do it right? Setting the mood is a big part of being passionate lovers, so let us make this kitchen hot and spice it up. Mom told us not to play with our food. Well, Mom's not here, so let's play and have fun. Remember, always planning this way can take time, so don't rush it.

Put two wineglasses in the refrigerator and chill a white wine, or set out some red wine to breathe. Time to dress up, or shall we say dress down. No boxers or the same old underwear she has seen you in. Put on a nice clean tank top and men's bikini underwear.

Put on nice cologne. Now, some perfumes are a turn on and some are more of a turn off. Plan ahead and ask her first what she likes in men's cologne. Have her put on a nice sexy teddy that will set her mind to be in a sexy mood. So you two will not get burned, or have food stains, have his and hers cooking aprons on, which will add a little fun.

You are setting the mood for her, and when you do this, you'll drive her wild. Now you need to be setting the mood before she even sees you. Call her and tell her how much she turns you on and that you'd like to have a special night with her, and you want to make hot, passionate love to her.

You are raising her libido and stimulating her mind as she imagines what a hot night you will give her. Do this before you even start stimulating her body. Set the table before she comes over, and have two candles on the table already lit. Have nice slow music on because you are setting the mood, and it will set your mood, too.

WARNING:
DON'T KILL HER MOOD

DO NOT say anything to your partner about her body. Too fat, too skinny, out of shape... THIS WILL KILL THE MOOD. YOUR NIGHT IS OVER!

Cooking with each other is a good way to play. As you are fixing the food...feed each other with your fingers. Pour each of you a cold glass of wine. Give her a sip. You can dip a finger into your wine...then let her suck it off your finger. What do you think she's thinking as she is sucking the wine off your finger? You want to keep stimulating her mind.

Then give her a light, stimulating kiss. Whisper something dirty to her. You don't need to talk like a porn star, just a little something. You are getting her in the mood. Only a man can release that potential in his woman.

If you have children, it's time for Grandma or a babysitter. Get the children out of the house tonight. You are rated—X—with a long night ahead of you. You don't want to stay in the kitchen all night.

You want to fix something light to eat because you don't want to overeat. Then you are too full to do anything but sleep.

JUST A LITTLE FOREPLAY

Make preparations for a night of passionate lovemaking. Make it an event for her and you. Have her on the sofa with soft music playing and candles lit. Spend 30 to 45 minutes just kissing and caressing her body. Give her the romance she hungers for and the heat she's been craving from you. Now slowly stroke her body with your fingertips.

Instead of jumping the gun and diving in for the kill, resist the urge to have sex; you want to take her to the bedroom for that. Slowly work her up to it. You are raising her libido and stimulating her mind as you whisper the things you want to do to her body, giving her mental foreplay.

STIMULATING TOUCH

You are making her fantasize about what you will be doing to her in the bedroom, and as you do this her body is becoming more sexually responsive to your touch. Sex and foreplay do not start in the bedroom. Stimulating foreplay should never start when you get in the bed. You want to do this before the bedroom.

This is your make-out time as you start to give her a little stimulating foreplay. Do not make the mistake of digging your fingers deep into her vagina. Touching is essential before any penetration, as it allows enough time for arousal as well as vaginal lubrication.

You need to start slowly at the top of her clitoris and very slowly, with just your fingertips, give her clitoris stimulation. Now, her clitoris has a central role in elevating her feelings. During her sexual excitement, her clitoris will swell and change position.

The blood vessels through the whole pelvic area also swell, causing engorgement and creating a feeling of fullness and sexual sensitivity.

Now her inner vaginal lips will swell and change shape. Keep in mind you are only working at the top of her clitoris. You still have her vagina to play with, too. Having great sex requires great stimulating foreplay.

Stimulating her is what you want to do before you take her to the bedroom. This is to give her first a clitoral orgasm.

As you are passionately French kissing her, you need to give her a little tease. Run your tongue all the way down her front, opening up her legs, and slowly start kissing between her legs. Her vagina will balloon upward as if to say, Here I am, suck on me, lick me, take me, make me cum, and this is where you will be stimulating her to the brink of her first orgasm. Remember, you are just stimulating her. Slow down and enjoy the night. Her clitoris is a very sensitive organ. It has between 6,000 to 8,000 nerve endings.

PASSIONATE LOVEMAKING

As you take her to your bedroom, she can see you only by candlelight. In the bedroom always keep your window a little open for ventilation. Have soft music in the background. Feed the two of you strawberries or some kind of fruit, and chilled wine will top it off.

Slowly undress one other. Start giving her long, hot, wet, deep, passionate kisses. As you feed her strawberries, keep kissing her. As you're kissing her lips, her neck, and her ears, whisper to her and tell her how sexy she is, and how much she turns you on. Let her know how much you want her tonight.

"MENTAL FOREPLAY"

Whisper something sexy and a little dirty to her. You want to give her mental foreplay. In fact, with mental foreplay you are sexually stimulating her mind. Mental stimulation, I feel, is very critical at this point.

You want to bring out that primal, animal side of her, which will makes her entire experience so much more exciting. You want to affect her mentally and emotionally. As you are whispering in her ear, kiss her ear because this is a sensitive hot spot that is sure to quickly stimulate her. You need to understand that many women actually like dirty talk from their men. Now, understand there is a time and place for everything.

As you are kissing her, you will hear her moan, and now you know she's getting hot as you are telling her what you want to do to her body. You want to keep the fire going, keeping her hot and mentally stimulating her with more passionate kissing. Just because you are in bed, don't stop giving her mental foreplay.

"HIGHLY CHARGED EROTIC PLACE"

Moving down to her neck, this is one of the most sensuous spots of a woman's body. She will experience a great deal of pleasure from you. Breathe your warm breath over her neck as you are kissing, sucking, and licking her. Some women have had orgasms from passionate kissing and sucking in this area; you are working her body as well as her mind.

As you do this, you are stimulating her mind. This is something a lot of men don't understand. They don't realize how powerful our minds are. Just by whispering to her, you are mentally stimulating and giving her thoughts of sexual excitement, something a lot of men will leave out. This is where you want to keep raising her libido to a slow boil. You want to explore every area of her body as you are kissing her. Move down her neck to start kissing her breasts. This highly charged erotic place is where you can make a woman hot and elevate her feelings to more sexual arousal.

I'll give you examples of a girlfriend of mine that I have been dating. She was married two times. Both men were big men. One was over six-foot-four and muscle-bound, and the other again over six feet tall and nice-looking. Now, these guys had no clue how to stimulate her mind or her body at all. Both men were very boring in the bedroom. They both would start sex only in the bedroom; there was never any sexual stimulation.

I asked her how often she thought about sex with her husband. She said, "J.T., the only time I had sex was when he wanted it. Then it was over as fast as it started. I was very sexually frustrated in my relationships. I was thinking of sex a lot but not with my husband." She then told me, "Now with you, oh my God, I want to have sex with you more than any man I ever met. J.T., you know how to sexually arouse and excite me. It's like you have this power over my body and my mind."

SLOW DOWN WITH HER BREASTS

You want to start by gently kissing, stroking, and lightly sucking on her breasts and nipples. Sexually responsive nipples will harden, and that means she is highly aroused. Squeezing her breasts and gently biting her nipples can be exciting for her. In this area, slow down and do not rush. Men tend to be too rough with women's breasts. Never be afraid to ask her to tell you if you get too rough.

Lay her face down on the bed and start kissing her on the back of her neck. Slowly kiss and run your tongue down to the small of her back, where a woman's hot spot is located. Always give special attention to any of her sensitive areas and linger longer in those spots.

Slow down and have fun with it. Behind her leg to the inside of her thigh is highly sensitive. This is a hot spot, so take your time. Kissing and running your tongue over her body will give her a sexual awakening. Have fun with this as you explore every area of her body, and don't worry, she won't mind.

You want to do more kissing and playing here with your lips and your tongue. With just your fingertips, give her vaginal stimulation and foreplay from behind. Always take your time. Just because you two are in bed, it's far from over. You want to be in total and absolute control of what's going on with her.

GIVING HER PLEASURE

At this point set her up in doggy-style position, with her legs open. Start kissing her and biting her just a little. Her buttocks are richly pleasure-sensitive, and she will find this very exciting. Now run your tongue down to her vagina, giving her just a little oral sex.

She will be thinking you are going to penetrate her from behind, but don't. Move down to the inside of her thighs and start kissing and touching her. Giving her more stimulation, you are working each part of her body. Think of each part of her body as a completely new beginning.

Now lay her on her back and start kissing, caressing, and cuddling her. Begin kissing her lips, mouth, and giving her long, deep, hot, passionate French kisses. While kissing her neck and ears, slowly run your fingertips down the center of her body, lightly touching and stroking her. Allow your tongue to follow your fingertips when you get to a sensitive spot and linger longer.

WITH YOUR FINGERTIPS

Start working on her breasts by kissing, licking, squeezing, and sucking. As you do this, run your fingertips down between her legs and open them. At the top of her clitoris start giving her stimulating foreplay with your fingertips. You want to give her foreplay until she has her first of many orgasms. It becomes easier for her to orgasm a second and third time as long as she can stay sexually stimulated and fully aroused.

You can make climaxing very easy for her in this highly sensitive area. Understand, there is a lot more to sex than just the penetration. Foreplay is sex. As a man when we say sex, we are thinking only of intercourse. Intercourse is just one of the many things included in sex.

Women absolutely love stimulating foreplay. It is very pleasurable to them, and she will love the way you make her feel. Whisper and tell her she is beautiful and sexy. Make her feel desired by you. This would be a good time to give her a little dirty talk. I learned years ago that most women I have been with actually love some dirty talk. This is good to do in the heat of passion. I have seen that it will drive my woman wild and crazy with desire. At this time, she will want deep penetration from you, but hold off. Her clitoris will be aroused and ready for your tongue. If she feels too sensitive you can come back again later.

FOREPLAY WITH YOUR TONGUE

The best foreplay I experience with women is with the tongue. Tuck a pillow under her hips to elevate her pelvis upward so that it is easier for you to get to her vagina. There are no limits to the pleasure you will be giving her with cunnilingus. Let's face it; you want to help your lover reach the highest climax you can give her. Imagine how much more sex you'll enjoy together when you are giving her the most intense sexual pleasure through oral stimulation.

She will be more receptive to you giving her oral sex. The best foreplay is with your tongue. Oral sex is using your tongue to give your woman an orgasm that she will love. You want to take your time when giving her oral sex.

This will further her stimulation to her sensitive areas, which makes it easier for you to make her climax over and over again. Giving her gentle clitoral stimulation using just your tongue as you do this, open the lips of her vagina with your fingers and explore her with your tongue.

This area will swell, causing engorgement and creating a feeling of fullness and sexual sensitivity. You want to lick and suck on her clitoral area; this will give her pleasure as you give her a clitoral orgasm. At this time her reactions will be to arch back as she gasps for air. You are giving her a feeling of great pleasure with your tongue once she has had a clitoral orgasm. Move away and try not to stay in one spot too long because it will get boring for her. Now move to the walls of her vagina, working your tongue, and she will crave for you to perform oral sex over and over again. The two types of orgasms a woman can have are clitoral and G-spot (otherwise known as vaginal orgasms).

STIMULATE HER G-SPOT

For vaginal orgasms you want to give your partner pleasure with multiple orgasms, so move down to the vagina opening. As you do this, insert your two fingers (ring and middle) into her vagina, giving her the come here, baby, bending your fingers toward her belly. Inside of her vagina, you are working her upper wall.

The G-spot texture is ridged (not as smooth) and very spongy feeling. Now, stimulation will take a little longer and require you to put a little more effort into it. Slow down and do not rush. You will provide a far more intense orgasmic pleasure than she has ever had from you. You want to stimulate the clitoris and her vagina, both areas at the same time. I enjoy stimulating her clitoris with my tongue as I'm working her G-spot at the same time.

Giving her stimulation with fingers and tongue at the same time is a technique so incredible and powerful that she may release fluid through her urethra during this sexual activity. No, this is not urine. This is a female ejaculation. Enjoy giving her pleasure and complete sexual satisfaction that will make her tremble with excitement.

AFTER THE LOVEMAKING

One of the most common things I keep hearing from married and single women is when the lovemaking is over, it is all over and so is the man. When a man has his orgasm it's over for us until we get an erection again. When you are done, do not get up or leave her at all. Stay in bed with her.

What we as men need to understand is how we are making her feel. By getting up and leaving her, you are making her feel abandoned and alone, even betrayed by you. You have no idea what you are doing to her. Do not ignore her because it's not over for her. Now, if you need a little cleaning up then do so, but do not be too long because she's waiting for you. You can have a washcloth or a towel waiting for you, but continue communication, letting her know how much you enjoy her, how much you love her, how happy she makes you. Hold her and lightly stroke and touch her body. You two can take a little nap as you hold her and let her sleep in your arms.

If she has not finished reaching her orgasm, remember,

you can bring her there by giving her oral sex or using your fingers till she reaches her climax. Even if it's over for you it may not be for her, so don't stop. Stay with her and keep kissing her neck, her back, and buttocks.

Keep the feeling pleasurable for her. Whisper and tell her how much you enjoy her, lying close together holding her in your arms. You two can spoon together; this will provide close body contact, and it will give her a feeling of security.

BE DRIVEN TO SATISFY HER

You need to make her comfortable even after you two have been together for some time. Do not be doing the same old thing that she expects from you. A lot of women who have been married or together for a few years have told me that the man will do the same thing again and again. His moves are so old she knows every move he will do next.

They are not exciting at all. It's just like watching the same old boring re-run movie. You need to add a little spice to your old love life. One thing to remember is that sex does not start in the bedroom. Start out with a slow and soft kiss. One of the things I keep hearing is how women miss kissing. Start by giving her long, hot, wet, deep, passionate kisses. French kiss her slowly, deep kissing sensually with the kind of kiss that she needs to stop, just to catch her breath.

I am not saying you need to gag her with your tongue… far from that. This is where you need to be making out with her, just like when you two were dating. This is what women have been looking for in their life for years: that one special kind of man who has a deep desire and is driven totally to satisfy her sexual needs.

She is looking for someone who will succeed in satisfying all of her needs in bed. She is looking for you to be the kind of man who will drive her wild in bed. You must be the man who knows how to slow yourself down. Moreover, your only focus is to bring her to the biggest orgasm you can ever give a woman.

As men, we need to have the understanding that women love sex and want to have sex, not just plain boring sex that she knows she can get from any man out there today, but good sex, where you will be sexually satisfying and fulfill her needs in the bedroom, and she wants sex even more than you do.

You need to be in total and absolute control of what's going on. It is not about you going into the bedroom just to get yours and it's over. Let it be your driven goal and desire to fulfill her sexual needs.

Now as a man, you need to work her where she is just so hot and deeply wet, she is about to have her first orgasm before you get her to bed. That's what she's looking for from you.

TAKING HER FOR GRANTED

You can go to any dating web site and read the profile of what women are looking for. They are looking for a caring, passionate, romantic, and loving man who knows how to give them a night of hot, passionate lovemaking with exciting vaginal orgasms as you are taking care of her deepest sexual needs. If your woman is not getting the care and passion she is looking for from you, how long will it take before she looks for someone else?

The last time you took her to bed, did you romance her first? Did you sexually stimulate her? Did you do any of this before getting her into bed? Did you make out with her 30 minutes to an hour? Did you get her where she was so hot and dripping wet for you?

Would you make out with her if you two were together after ten years of marriage or dating? For a woman it's all about the passion and taking your time with her. This is why women will spend hours reading romance novels or watching soap operas. She needs to have her mind stimulated. This is why she will fantasize about having the hot, passionate sex in love and her life. She needs to get from you the passion, emotions, romance, and stimulation she is looking for as you fulfill her desires.

YOU MAKE HER
FEEL DESIRED

This is making her feel like you desire her. Yes, you still need to make out with her as if you two were dating. Even if you've been married ten, 20, or even 30 years, she is still a woman with needs and desires.

This is what she is hoping you will fulfill. This is what is missing if you've been with that person for a long time. After a few years, we are no longer trying to win our partner over. Now we see the one we love as a sister or, worse, a mother. We just take them for granted.

You lose your interest. No more are you dating her, no more cuddling with her, no more making time for her. You now see her as an old rug. She is just there.

Is this why some women are promiscuous and others are faithful? I was teaching a student one day when she started crying. Her crying was out of control; I asked her what was going on. As we began to talk, she told me about her marriage. She said, "I have been married for over twenty-three years to a police officer. We have two boys, twenty-one and nineteen, both in the army."

I said, "Wow, just like starting over. Kids are gone and you two are alone in the house, dating, going out, having fun with friends." She told me that it was not like that at all. She said her husband worked, came home, and sat in his recliner chair and watched TV until he fell asleep. He would leave her all alone on the big sofa to sit and cry.

As we talked, I could see how he did not understand. He was so comfortable in their relationship that he couldn't see how he was pushing her away. I asked her to do a little something for me. I told her to make a plan. "Go shopping, and pick a good white wine, get a sexy teddy, cook a little something for you two." I told her to do this to spark his interest. I could see it would be so easy for her to find a man because she was very nice-looking.

SETTING THE MOOD

A good way to start for a night of passionate lovemaking is to first set the mood. Make your plans. Always make time for her, seven days of the week. You need to set aside one or two nights a week for just the two of you. You do not need a lot of money to have a night of romance, just make a little time.

Think back to when you two were first dating and how you would make time for her. No matter how busy you were, you still made time and plans for her.

Now, after being married for a few years, guys will stop making any plans for having a night of intimacy, and this is one of the reasons why women can become bored and promiscuous; even a woman who loves her man and cares for him can wander.

She will look elsewhere for her sexual satisfaction because the sex at home is lame. It is up to you not to push her to go look for what is missing from you.

You are responsible for giving her a night of hot, passionate sex and lovemaking with exciting vaginal orgasms. You are taking care of her deepest sexual needs. In addition, if you make her feel good sexually in bed, she will want sex from you all the time; even more, she will plead to have sex with you. She will even be thinking of making love with you throughout the day.

Do this for a little fun. Take her to a lingerie store and pick out a sexy teddy, and let her pick out men's bikinis for you or what she thinks would be sexy on you.

This is your special girl, so treat her that way, and have fun. Start with setting the mood. As she is looking at lingerie, press your body up to hers and tell her how you cannot wait to get her home to relish her body.

Did you know the brain is the most powerful sex organ you have? You need to use it. With the right sexual frame of mind, you will add new sparks to your love life.

You need to be teachable and apply what you learn in this book to your love life. This will work, I know, because for years I have tried and tested everything I am telling you to do.

HER SEXUAL SATISFACTION

Always remember! Never start sex in the bedroom! One of the biggest mistakes is that men will not start any foreplay or vaginal stimulation until after they get her into the bedroom. Wrong! You need to slow down. Do not seduce your woman until after you get her into the bed—it's too late.

If the only time you start any sex is after you get her into the bedroom, then what does she have to look forward to from you? This will get boring with her, so don't assume this is exciting to her because it's not.

You are making her feel like she's just your sperm bank. You need to make her feel that she is wanted and desired by you. You need to give her the sexual awakening and vaginal stimulation she needs from you.

A planned night would be the best way to spark your love life. It's all about setting the mood from start to finish.

PULLING TEETH

I have two married friends whom I will refer to as Mike and Lorrie. They are a really nice couple. Mike loves his wife very much, and they are very happy with their two kids. They both have good jobs and a nice home. The only time they fight or disagree is when it comes time to have sex.

As much as Lorrie loves her husband, Mike, she hates having sex with him. Lorrie hates even thinking of having sex with her husband with a passion. Lorrie told me that sex with Mike is like pulling teeth. He does not even know where to start.

Mike would even beg his wife for sex and was often rejected, never understanding why. If a man would please his woman every time they had sex by giving her one, two, or three clitoral and vaginal orgasms, do you think a man would ever need to ask or beg for sex?

Lorrie is looking for a sexual awakening from her husband. Mike does not know how to make her feel like a woman in bed. Think of being married for a few years and every time you have sex it seems so mechanical and boring—you know every move that your partner will make.

MIKE WOULD CUM AND GO

One day I got a call from Mike to come over and talk with the two of them. Mike went out so Lorrie and I could talk. As Lorrie sat back and started talking with me, I could understand why their sex life was over. The relationship was cold. Lorrie said for years the only sex life Mike knew was just to drive it in, cum, get up, go watch TV, or go get something to eat.

Lorrie told me she was lucky if she was even fondled. She had never had an orgasm with Mike, and she was thinking about looking for a man to fulfill her sexual fantasy. She said that all women have needs. She was crying as she told me this. She was looking for the passion, the kissing, and the sexual stimulation she was not getting at home.

"I am not looking for a fuck," she said. "As a woman, I could get that from any man. I would love to be with a man who knows how to be romantic and to make mad, passionate love to me. If Mike would change and start giving me the passion, the romance, and the sexual stimulation, it would be like having a new husband." I could see from her viewpoint how right she was. I was thinking of the thousands of Mikes and Lorries out in the world today, crying and looking for the passion and romance that are gone from the marriage. This is why setting the mood is so important.

THE LIVING ROOM

This can be a very hot spot for you two to have fun and enjoy each other, not just a place to hang out with friends and watch TV and eat popcorn. This is your love nest, your home, and this can be your playtime. Sorry, it is time for your friends to go home—television off and candles on. It's playtime!

Time for you two to have a date night, some alone time where you can get very physical and have fun all night. You must always set your plans ahead for nights like this. Start by going out to a nice dinner, and while you two are waiting to be seated whisper something sexual and stimulating in her ear.

You are arousing her by giving her foreplay in her mind. You must build her up for her first orgasm so you'll now be putting thoughts in her mind. You are getting her in the mood.

Remember, our brain is a very powerful sex organ. You need to work and stimulate this part of her body. First, you want her to be thinking of how good it will be tonight when you make passionate love to her.

When your drinks and food come to your table, feed her a little with your fingers. As you feed her, kiss her lips, kiss and nibble on her neck. She knows people are watching, so this will be more exciting to her. Then whisper and talk a little dirty to her; you can tell her how much she excites you and how sexy she is. It's all about you making her feel like a hot and sexy woman.

You are putting the fire and passion back into your relationship. Most men and women will cheat because of the lack of the fire and passion in the relationship. Now, at this time you could give her a card or a red rose. Tonight she is not the homemaker, wife, or mom but a very sexy and attractive woman who is your date. When you get to the car, open the car door for her. This is something we always need to do.

In the car, give her a slow, deep, passionate kiss to raise her libido and stimulate her mind. Make out with her a little before going home. Tonight, your job is to see her as your girlfriend, not as your wife. Yes, this is just like role-playing. You need to see her as your new girlfriend and not your wife.

LET'S DANCE

Remember, after you get home, you are setting the mood for your super date night. Take her into your living room, cut the lights down low, and light some candles. Play some slow music, pour the two of you something to drink.

Take her in your arms and caress her body as you do this slow dance with her. You don't have to be a good dancer. She doesn't care. Now, hold her very close in your arms and slow dance with her.

Very slowly just move your bodies together as one with the music, kiss her neck, move, and keep your lips close to her ear. Whisper how much you love her. Your voice can be just as much pleasure to her as a kiss or a touch. Tell her how much her body gives you pleasure, and how happy you are just to be with her, and thank her, yes, thank her, for just being her.

LET HER SING TO YOU

Play some music that she knows, like one of the songs you both like. Ask her if she'll sing to you and slowly kiss her neck, her ear, her face, and her lips as she sings to you.

Now at this time kiss her with your tongue, letting your tongue dance with hers. Don't push it; you want to prolong your night. Let her anticipate your every move. For this will make it more exciting for her.

This will make it more physically satisfying for her and for you. You are making her want you more. You don't want to rush in, so take your time and make it last. You have all night. This is why planning is everything.

Just enjoy holding her as you move your bodies slowly to the music. From my viewpoint, as a dance instructor, I have seen and been told by hundreds of women how sexy it is to see a man slow dance. And watch him move his body with the music as well.

NOT OTHER MEN'S JOB
TO ENTERTAIN HER

I have seen men take their wives /girlfriends out dancing but not dance with her. As a guy you don't ever want to do that. You don't want to put candy in front of a baby, then tell the baby they can't have it.

Now, this same man will get upset if any guy asks her to dance, thinking he might lose her to another man. However, at the same time he won't get up to even try to dance with her.

Ask yourself this: would you go out hoping to have fun and a good time when someone then tells you to just sit down and have a good time? It would be more fun for you to dance with her than for you to sit and watch other men dancing with her and giving her the excitement she's waiting for from you.

She is having fun with other men and not you. She needs the physical and mental attention from you. It is up to you to give her the physical excitement she is looking for.

It's not the job of other men to entertain your wife /girl-friend…it is your job!

On the other hand, take her out dancing and have fun. You two dance together, laugh with each other, and make it fun for you and her. Hold her hand, ask the DJ to play a slow song, then slow dance with her and make it fun.

CAN YOU FEEL
THE HEAT AND
THE PASSION OF
THE MUSIC?
YOUR BODIES
PRESSED
TIGHTLY
TOGETHER.
MOVE YOUR
BODIES TO THE
RHYTHM OF THE
MUSIC.

SOMETHING TO THINK ABOUT

I had a friend who was a nice guy and who was married to a very nice-looking woman with a very nice-looking body. She would stay home and do the cooking, laundry, house-keeping, and look after his two kids from his previous marriage. He would go to work and she would stay home.

He was overlooking what he had in this very beautiful woman. She was very lonely without the physical, sexual, and mental attention she needed from him. He would work, come home, eat, take his shower, clean up, and then he would go out with the boys to play pool or have happy hour. Sometimes he would be out until 4 a.m., leaving her alone so many times without even a kiss good-bye.

When he was dating her, there wasn't anything he would not do to win her love. Now what would he do to keep her love? You must always show her the physical and sexual attention she needs from you. So many of us will get married or be in a relationship and after a few years, it is over.

ONE MAN'S HOUSEKEEPER IS ANOTHER MAN'S TREASURE

We do not see what we are missing. You are not interested in satisfying her needs as a woman. Do you know how many men out there would love to have the opportunity to be with your woman? There are so many men out there who would give their right arms to have what you have. They would not see her as you see her now. Maybe she doesn't look to you like she did when you were first married. Well, you probably don't look the same to her either, but you can count on the fact that she may be attractive to other men.

Remember my friend? He came home from work to get ready for a big pool tournament. When he opened his door and walked into his house he saw his wife was not home, there was no hot meal, and no clean house. This beautiful woman, who he only saw as his housekeeper and the woman who looked after his two kids, was not home waiting for him.

It was all over. She moved out because she had had it; it was all over for her. It seems that some men will never get it. He had no clue that he had all the opportunity to spend time with her.

SOMETIMES WE NEED
A LITTLE TEASE

BEFORE IT'S TIME
TO PLEASE

JUST AS A MOTH IS
DRAWN TO THE FLAME

SHE WILL BE
DRAWN TO YOU

COMMUNICATION IS
VERY IMPORTANT

Now, just like a wood stove, if you don't keep watching and working, the fire will go out. Your love is that wood stove. You need to tend to its needs all of the time. Do this! For you and your girl on your day off, wake up a little early, slide out of bed, and fix the two of you a little breakfast. Don't go overboard. You're cooking just a little something to eat together. Feed each other, then sit and talk. Yes, talk and have your cup of coffee or tea. We are in a fast-paced world. Some people forget how to just sit down and relax and talk. Communication is very important with any and all relationships. This is what we forget to do.

LOST FOR WORDS
OUTSIDE OF A WEB SITE

This will give you some physical closeness before your day begins. Eye contact is always a plus. I met a woman on a date site and we hit it off. We would chat and text for hours. We would chat from 9 p.m. until 4 a.m. Then I asked her to meet me for coffee at the coffee shop.

The day came and we met. We got our coffee and sat down to talk. Right away I knew it was over because I could see that she could not communicate outside of a web site. I kept trying to talk to her, but she was lost for words. You see, her communication skills did not go past the Internet or texting. At one time she asked me, "Can I go get my laptop?" I said, "This date is over." As you can see, this woman could not carry on a conversation, so I knew we would not have much of a relationship without communication.

As you two have so much more to talk about in your marriage or in your relationship, one of the first things to end is your skill to communicate with one another. Don't let this happen. Remember, keep tending to the wood stove's needs or the fire will go out, only to be relit by a new lover.

For the next 30 days do something new and exciting for her. Get your mind set on dating. Make plans if you are dating or married. Remember, she is the desire of your heart.

Do the little things that will make a big difference in your lives. Start doing new things, like going out for a bike ride, a walk in the park, a long drive, or out for a cup of coffee. Talk to her about her job, her mom, where she'd like to be in the next five years, her fantasies, just something. Keep your communication alive.

Keep the communication open and ask her what she likes from you in bed. This is what couples are leaving out and not talking to each other about. The more you know about pleasing her in bed, the more she will come back to you.

Think of this: she's giving you oral sex, and it doesn't do anything for you. In fact, it's bad, and you don't like it at all. She's thinking that you love what she is doing. Unless you talk to her about it, how will she know if she's doing good or bad?

It will stay the same. This is why all communication is so very important. I had a friend who would go out and pay a prostitute to give him oral sex when all he had to do was tell his wife what he did and did not like from her regarding giving him oral sex. Just talking to her keeps your communication open. Think of the fun you can have by showing and teaching her what feels good when she's giving you oral sex.

(WARNING)

Don't ever pay a prostitute for any sex, ever. You can get an STD and you will lose the one you love. You can, and will, go to jail. You are responsible for your actions, not her. Do not let your line of communication be your weaknesses that will stand between the two of you.

A very successful marriage has a strong line of communication. The possibilities of what you two can do and have are endless. Take five or ten minutes, sit in bed, and think only of the positive things you two have in each other and what a great day you will have. Now think of everything you have to be grateful for.

Look deep into one another's eyes and speak only of the positive things you see in one another. Don't see, don't think, and don't even speak anything that is negative. Stay positive.

This is teaching you to change your mind-set. Move from the negative and focus on the positive and what you want your day to be like. You two are now telling the universe how your day will be, saying, "I will have a positive day." What a way to start out a new day, by taking action with the positive before your day starts. You two are now starting out with a positive day.

AUTO-SUGGESTION

Auto-suggestion is the medium for influencing your sub-conscious mind, and to teach you to stop looking at your glass as half empty instead of half full. Let us say your glass of life is half empty, and say in your subconscious mind today my glass will be full.

If you can see it in your mind's eye, you will hold it in your hand. The simple principles you are using to influence your subconscious mind are so easy. We make it harder than it is to change our mind-set from the negative world we have made for ourselves.

Move into the positive way of thinking. Moreover, stop thinking and influencing your life with the negative. Only think and talk of the positive. Then you will see things in your life change.

I had a student who I was teaching Latin and ballroom dancing. He was the worst student I ever had in all my 20-some years of teaching ballroom dance. He was a beginner dance student who was always trying to tell me what and how to teach my dance class.

I did not enjoy even teaching my own class with him, and I was the teacher. I could see how I was holding onto all the negative energy, which I was putting out. When I changed my mind-set, I saw my student change as well.

CHANGING YOUR MIND
WILL CHANGE PEOPLE

You see, I stopped looking for the negative or the things that I did not want and started looking for and focusing on the positive and the things I did want. I was using auto-suggestion to communicate to the object of my desire by influencing my own thoughts.

Thoughts will attract things into your life if you keep thinking of what you don't want to show up. Bad or good, you will draw them into your life. You need to stop and train your thoughts.

This is very easy to do. Think of a boxer. Before he busts into the ring for a prizefight he will be psyching himself out to win the fight. As you can see before he even gets into the ring, he has won the fight. He is using auto-suggestion to influence his own mind.

How does this play into your relationship? Ask yourself, what do you want from your spouse or your girlfriend in your relationship? Think as if you have it in the now, not in the past tense, but in the present tense. Think of what a great love life you two have and hold onto the good thoughts, like a burning desire of passionate love. Make it clear what you want. Moreover, you will have it. Keep using the law of attraction in your relationship and your life. Auto-suggestion has a lot to do with this.

DON'T GET TOO COMFORTABLE

In our day-to-day life sometimes we get too comfortable, just like sleeping in too late, and as good as it sounds, this can be bad. You wake up late and half of your day is over. Don't get behind the eight ball because it will run you over. We know if we don't cut the grass, the weeds will take over our flower bed.

I had a friend who worked out in a gym every day. He had a body like a Greek god. I asked him why he worked out at the gym every day so hard. He told me that if he slowed down he would lose what he had worked so hard to get, and His body would get out of shape.

This is like your relationship; if we leave it alone, the weeds of life will and can take over. She will be bored and lose interest in you. This can happen to anyone without exception. Just like eating the same foods every day, even a good steak after some time will get boring. However, there are hundreds of ways to prepare that same steak to add a little spice and fire to that boring steak.

The love you are bored with today can be your fire and your passion for tomorrow. So many times, we as men have misunderstood the meaning of being in a relationship. We have no clue after we have been with our wife or girlfriend for years.

When the newness of the relationship wears off, what do we do? It seems we work hard just to win her love, and then we blow it by doing nothing to keep it. Think back when you two were dating and you felt so much in love. You had great communication with each other.

You had so much in common, and you made time for her. You two were a team; you would think and daydream about her, make plans together just to be with her. Now it's like you are in two different worlds. You used to have so much to talk about, but now you have to dig deep just to think of something to say. This can be fixed by simply changing your mind-set.

Get out of the old rut you've been in and start over; you need to take the lead. Start doing new things together. This is a new start. Treat her like you were dating her. If all you do after work is watch TV till it's time for bed or play on the PC, then change it. Start doing new things with her like going to the movies. See something funny or ask her to pick the movie. Do not stay at home, GO OUT! Hold her hand, feed her popcorn, go out with some friends, play some games together, go hiking, take a class together, or take a dance lesson. There is so much you can do, and a lot of things are free.

It is all about spending time together and having fun. This will give you something in common. The key reason for not talking is not having anything in common. Did we forget why we got married? To live and love forever, not just through the good times but the bad times as well. We need to go back to the beginning, back to the drawing board where it all began.

STARTING OVER

Now, before you take your wife or girlfriend to bed, makes plans hours or even days ahead to set the mood. Just like when you two were first dating, when you would make things just right for her with music, flowers, your cologne, food, and drinks. Everything had to be just right, and you would do all you could just to make her happy.

You would do anything for her. So why does it need to stop after you two are married or you've been together for years?

Keep this in mind. The same fire and passion you had with her before, you can have again. You can and you will have it again. It is up to you to keep it going.

Think of it as just like starting over. This is why after being with someone for some time, the fun, excitement, and passion are gone. This is why women will get sexually frustrated in their relationship and lose any interest in having sex with you. You are no longer trying to keep it alive. You can start over by adding and doing new things.

Start trying new things. This is not that hard to do. Just a little of your time and make it fun. You can go to the store and buy one or two red roses and pick off the petals. Then put the rose petals all over the sheets and the pillows, and have three or four candles lit, nice chilled white wine, and soft music. It's the little things you are doing to add the spark to your boring love and sex life. You must keep it alive because it's like anything, if you don't use it you will lose it.

THE LOVE YOU
ARE BORED
WITH TODAY

WILL BE THE FIRE
AND PASSION
OF SOMEONE

TOMORROW

FOREPLAY AND LESS COMPUTER PLAY

I met a very nice-looking Russian woman who we will call Margie. She was very beautiful and she had very long legs, sexy blue eyes, blond hair, and she was built like a model. She had a job working with a big law firm, and she was going to school at night to be a lawyer.

This girl was a man magnet. I could see how men could fall for her. As she and I sat and talked, she was crying about her husband. He was in the Navy. I was thinking, Navy man, okay, he is gone out to sea six months to a year, and she is missing him. But as it turned out he was always home because he had shore duty.

She began to tell me that they had only been married for five years. Then she told me how lonely she was. She said he would come in from work and play all night with his games on the computer. I could not help but think what a loser this man was.

She told me she bought a very sexy teddy to spice things up in the bedroom because she was thinking how much he would like it. She said when she tried to show him, he would not take his eyes off his games even to look at her.

"He makes me feel so unwanted. I'm no longer his focus, or his desire. He does not understand me as a woman. I have needs and wants, too. I do not ask for his money, because I have a job and a car. All I want from him is to be held and cuddled and to feel wanted and desired. I need the passion and the stimulation by him. Why must the fire and the passion stop after we get married?"

As you can see, he was too comfortable with his wife, and more so, his Margie was no longer the woman of his dreams. Now as a guy, lying around the house and doing nothing will not keep the fire and the passion going. This is why it's so important to be working on your relationship. Having this book to read and to apply to your life will help you.

COOKING

When she cooks for you, you need to let her know how much you appreciate her and how much you appreciate her cooking for you, how she makes you feel, and how much you love eating her cooking.

Don't wait hours after you finish eating your dinner. When you are done eating, do the dishes, or put them in the dishwasher to help her. Now would be a good time to go over to her and just hold her in your arms and say thank you. Then you can make the two of you a little coffee, dessert, or something to drink.

The point is showing her how much you appreciate her. Those five minutes of her being in your arms will mean so much to her. Sometimes we will give the dog more attention when he runs to fetch a ball than when she cooks or cleans the house all day.

I have seen so many men who will proclaim their love only with their lips and do nothing to show it. Any man can do this. You must set yourself apart from the rest, and stand up and show your love.

Seldom do we take the time from our busy lives to devote ourselves as much time to keep winning her heart after we are married or we are dating her. Just like the little child who asks their mom and dad for a pet, saying that they will take care of it, feed it, clean up after it, and after a short while, it stops.

In this book, you have read true stories of people that I have helped out in their love and sex life.

It is up to you to keep the fire, and the passion, going. It is up to you not to let it slowly die. I just hope you will use some of the key principles in this book to help you.

I'm Joe Tango.

She will thank you.

CPSIA information can be obtained at www.ICGtesting.com
Printed in the USA
BVOW08s1432021213

337918BV00001B/184/P